DIGITAL AND INFORMATION LITERACY ™

BLOGGER OR JOURNALIST?
EVALUATING WHAT IS THE PRESS IN THE DIGITAL AGE

TRACY BROWN

rosen publishing's
rosen
central

New York

For Liam and Frances, who feature in my work as both a journalist and blogger

Published in 2013 by The Rosen Publishing Group, Inc.
29 East 21st Street, New York, NY 10010

Library of Congress Cataloging-in-Publication Data

Brown, Tracy.
Blogger or journalist?: evaluating what is the press in the digital age/Tracy Brown. — 1st ed.
      p. cm. — (Digital and information literacy)
Includes bibliographical references and index.
ISBN 978-1-4488-8358-5 (library binding) —
ISBN 978-1-4488-8364-6 (pbk.) —
ISBN 978-1-4488-8365-3 (6-pack)
1. Citizen journalism. 2. Online journalism. 3. Journalism–Objectivity. 4. Social media. 5. Blogs. I. Title.
PN4784.C615B86 2013
302.23 — dc23

                                                                    2012024921

Manufactured in the United States of America

CPSIA Compliance Information: Batch #W13YA: For further information, contact Rosen Publishing, New York, New York, at 1-800-237-9932.

CONTENTS

INTRODUCTION

The days of relying on the newspaper delivery boy to deliver information to households are long over. The Internet and mobile phone technologies have changed how information is gathered and delivered in ways that can't be overstated. They have allowed people worldwide to gather, share, and access news as it's happening. The Internet and sites such as Facebook and YouTube have made it possible for anyone to reach a broad, global audience and for anyone with a computer to be a news provider.

There is an enormous amount of content available online, on just about any topic. Viewers and readers must weed through this information to find sources that they trust and that they can rely on, in the same way that people read their daily paper or watch their favorite television news broadcast.

The difference is the people who write for newspapers or television news are journalists—people whose job it is to research and deliver news to the public. When you go online, you find content from lots of different people, many of whom are not actual journalists, but interested citizens who want to share information with the public, much like journalists do.

These non-journalists include writers of blogs and producers of independent news stories—people who are not working for official media outlets like established news channels or publications.

Technology has made the world a smaller place by enabling anyone with a computer or telephone and Internet access to communicate events and share images around the globe instantly.

Here, we will look at the differences between journalists and this new breed of news providers. We will discuss what professional standards journalists must follow that bloggers are not bound to, as well as what laws protect journalists but do not offer the same protection for non-journalists. Also discussed will be the roles different types of news providers serve in society, and how our definition of journalism is changing.

The purpose is to help consumers of online news better understand where the news they read is coming from, what news they can trust, how to tell the difference between fact and opinion, and how to put together everything they read to form their own ideas about current events—and then perhaps even to share their ideas in their own online publications or blogs.

Chapter 1

Understanding the Role of a Journalist

Where do you turn to find out who won your local town hall election or when your favorite band will release another album? Whether you are interested in politics, fashion, sports, or any other topic, you likely rely at least in part on journalists to learn what's happening.

A journalist is a person whose job it is to investigate and report the news. Journalists go directly to the source of news—politicians, celebrities, or anyone who does anything that is newsworthy—and deliver the story to the public. The men and women who write articles for your local paper are journalists. The people you see reading the news on television are also journalists, as are the people who read the news on the radio.

It would be much more difficult to know what was going on in the world if we did not have journalists. Imagine if you had to call the manager of your favorite baseball team to learn who would be the starting shortstop in the next game or if you had to fly around the world to follow elections in faraway countries.

Journalists do the research and investigating for you. They seek out the facts and talk to the people who can best inform the world about what's

President Barack Obama waves to the crowd after giving a speech at the University of North Carolina in Chapel Hill in 2012. Internet technologies make it possible for such events to be broadcast around the world.

happening with a particular topic or person. They have contacts and connections that most people do not have, and they can learn about interesting events and outcomes as they happen. All we have to do then is read or listen to their reports to keep informed.

We put a lot of trust in journalists to cover important events and to tell us the truth about what is happening in the world. Let's take a look at the important role journalists play and at the professional standards that are in place to keep journalists trustworthy.

File   Edit   View   Favorites   Tools   Help

ELEMENTS OF JOURNALISM

Elements of Journalism

Journalists have a big responsibility, and the public puts a lot of trust in them to do their jobs well. Professional, honest journalism requires certain elements, including:

Journalism should tell the truth. A journalist's number one goal should be to report the news accurately and fairly.

Journalists are loyal to the people. A journalist serves the public— a journalist should not work to protect his or her subjects but to deliver important news to the people.

Journalism means verifying facts. A journalist cannot assume anything is true without checking it. Research and verification are key. A journalist must be very thorough.

Journalists are independent from those they cover. When journalists are writing about a person or company, for example, they should not feel they have to say nice things about that person or company. They are impartial, which means they do not take sides.

Journalists must be independent observers of power. A journalist's job is to investigate and report on the actions of people in power, and a journalist should do so without feeling swayed by the powerful people he or she is reporting on. This means a journalist should not be intimidated by people in power in a way that discourages him or her from investigating and sharing information that may reveal bad things about someone in power.

Ethical Standards

Not just anyone can be a journalist, just as not everyone can take on the role of a policewoman or lawyer without the correct qualifications. To become a journalist, a person must usually earn a college degree and be employed by an official news source. Journalists work for a particular publication, including newspapers, magazines, and Web sites, as well as television news networks. Some journalists work full-time for a particular news source, while others are hired to cover only certain stories for one news source.

A professional journalist has to follow certain rules or standards that are set by other journalists and journalistic organizations. These rules have

Print and broadcast journalists have a responsibility to public citizens to be truthful and unbiased in the news they deliver, and thorough and balanced in the reporting they do.

to do with how news is researched and reported, and how journalists get their information and what they decide to share.

For example, journalists agree to follow rules that protect the people who are the subject of a story. This means not giving the names of children who are involved in a news event, for example, or being sensitive about printing or sharing photographs that may be disturbing or offensive.

Although there is no one set of codes or rules for journalists—different publications, organizations, and even countries have varying ethical codes for journalists—most say more or less the same thing. In a nutshell, a journalist should be truthful, objective, impartial, and fair.

Truthfulness

A journalist must agree to tell the truth. This may sound obvious, but it's a very important standard. It doesn't just mean that the journalist won't lie in the story but that the journalist will do his or her best to tell the full story.

Not every story has only one truth. Sometimes a story is about an argument that has not yet been decided but in which both sides have valid points. Say, for example, kids in your community want to build a skateboarding ramp in a vacant lot in your town, but nearby homeowners are against it because it will be too noisy. A journalist can't just report the story from the homeowners' or from the kids' point of view. That would not be the complete story. The journalist will do whatever he or she can to be sure the story is told from all sides.

A journalist has to do more than just repeat what he or she has been told. A journalist's job is to question, investigate, and share all positions of an argument without taking sides. This means being very diligent in research and in finding reliable sources—people who are qualified to speak about a particular issue—to share their points of view.

Objectivity

In the skateboarding ramp example, a good journalist will report what others think is the right course of action without revealing what he or she thinks. A journalist must not share his or her own ideas or opinions in a story—the journalist's job is to report the facts. If a journalist is one of the homeowners who are against the skateboarding ramp being built, it would be unethical for him or her to write an article only from the point of view of people who don't want the ramp built.

The stories that journalists deliver to the public can influence how the public responds to a certain issue, and it is unethical for a journalist to use this power to get something he or she wants.

Accountability

Being accountable to the public—the reader—is very important for practicing good journalism. A journalist can't just make up stories or parts of stories. He or she cannot manipulate facts to mislead the public about what

Journalists are trusted to write the truth, be able to support facts they publish, and be able to identify any sources they rely on to get information for a story.

is happening. A good journalist has to be ready to defend his or her work. If someone questions whether a person quoted in a story really said what was printed, the journalist has to be able to show that the quote is accurate. Inventing sources, changing facts, or plagiarizing—copying someone else's writing—are unethical practices in journalism.

Just as the public trusts doctors to have a patient's best interest at heart when practicing medicine, journalists must be trusted to serve the public honestly. Having professional rules and ethical codes is a good reminder to journalists of their responsibility to the public.

Journalists are only human, of course, and mistakes do happen. Most publications have a corrections section where errors are admitted and fixed. For example, a person may have been misquoted in an earlier article, or a name or date may have been incorrectly given in a piece of writing. Making a mistake is not unethical as long as you acknowledge and correct it.

Chapter 2

Bloggers, Tweeters, and Other Opinion Posters

Imagine having to wait for the six o'clock news to find out what caused a fire in your town or whether it will snow tomorrow. Now consider having to wait several days for a letter from a faraway cousin to arrive in your mailbox, letting you know how her vacation was.

In an age when we can text, e-mail, tweet, blog, and rely on social networking sites to share and get information, it's very hard to remember that not so long ago, none of these tools existed.

The impact of the Internet on how we gather, share, and process information has been staggering. Endless streams of content are now available, twenty-four hours a day, around the globe. If something happens somewhere, we can all know about it—we just have to wait as long as it takes for someone to go online and share.

The ease and speed with which anyone with a mobile phone or computer can share information means there is an endless vat of content available

New media, as opposed to traditional forms of print media like newspapers and magazines, enable anyone to share ideas or images in real-time, and to comment on ideas or images other people share.

online. People share photos, links to articles and videos, and thoughts and opinions that range from lengthy blog posts to off-the-cuff tweets, voicing their ideas in 140 characters or less.

Impact on Traditional Media

"Traditional media" is a term for newspapers, magazines, radio programs, and television broadcasts that existed before the Internet age. These are the tools through which information used to be almost entirely gathered and shared. If you lived in a particular city, you likely had just a few locally published newspapers to choose from. Although cable television news channels such as Fox and CNN changed how people got their news from television—by making news available twenty-four hours a day—people still relied on these programs to inform them of world and local events.

The Internet has changed all of this. For one thing, information on the Internet is, for the most part, freely accessible—people don't have to pay for it. In contrast, people do have to pay for most print publications and for access to cable television.

Because news was not free in the pre-Internet days, the production and delivery of news was a business, just like any other. Newspapers had to make money in order to stay in business. Journalists had to earn salaries from their work in order to support their families. The costs of printing and distributing a daily newspaper or a weekly or monthly magazine are staggering

Traditional media sources, such as CNN, compete with each other to be the first news outlet to "break" or deliver a story.

compared with the cost of setting up a Web site. Producing television news is also very expensive.

In addition to subscription fees to cover these costs, many news sources relied on advertising revenue—money earned by selling space on a page or time during a television or radio broadcast that companies could use to advertise their products or services. As people began turning to free online news sources, they were less willing to pay for traditional media sources, which also meant fewer companies wanted to spend money advertising through these channels.

The Internet age has seen the closure and bankruptcy of hundreds of daily newspapers in the United States alone. Many print publications have responded by coming up with paid subscription packages for online content. But it's too soon to tell whether the public, now used to online information being free, is willing to pay for it.

In some cases, it depends on how loyal readers are to a particular news publication. For example, if a person has been reading the *New York Times* for twenty years and now prefers to access his or her favorite columnists' pieces online, it's possible that reader will be willing to pay for the content rather than see the newspaper go bankrupt and have to shut down.

File   Edit   View   Favorites   Tools   Help

MEDIA BIAS

Media Bias

Although news sources are supposed to be unbiased and fair in their coverage of events, most have what is called an editorial slant that does impact how certain events are covered. For example, Fox News claims to be "fair and balanced," when in fact a large percentage of its programming is produced by individuals sharing their own personal opinions and viewpoints.

There are newspapers and television news programs that are more liberal than others and some that are more conservative. Point of view can make readers and viewers very loyal to the content produced by a particular news source. At the same time, editorial bias makes many news consumers— readers and viewers of the news—distrust mainstream traditional media.

The Rise of Web Logs

Mistrust of traditional media has encouraged many readers to seek out other news sources that are not tied to advertising sales or editorial slant, including nontraditional media, like blogs.

"Blog" is short for a "Web log"—a term that refers to the original purpose of blogs, which was a sort of Web journal or diary that some people kept online. Blogs sprung up all over the Internet, covering topics like people's pets, holidays, children, and hobbies. Today, people still blog for personal reasons, but many blogs have become more sophisticated, and many bloggers have turned their online writing into full-time jobs.

Blogs are written in a series of entries called posts, and posts usually appear on a blog in chronological order, with the most recent post appearing on the top. Blogs are usually interactive, which means that readers can leave comments in response to a post, and these comments are published on the blog for the public to see.

This kind of so-called interactive journalism allows the writer of a post to communicate directly with his or her readers. The blogger can clarify statements, defend arguments, or even admit when a commenter makes a good point. And because blogs are published online only, a blogger can revise, edit, or update a post at anytime, unlike a published article, which is permanently "out there" in black and white.

The Expanding Role of the Blogger

Blogging enables people to express their ideas and voice their points of view without having to go through the filter of an editor. Bloggers don't need to pitch their ideas to editors in order to get their stories published, like reporters who write for traditional media do. Anyone can download free and easy-to-use blogging software and begin publishing their own words.

Many professional journalists also have their own blogs, and many other professional bloggers are hired by reputable, well-known publications to write blogs. In these cases, editors are involved in shaping the content.

Anyone with a computer and Internet access can share knowledge, present ideas, and express opinions to a wide audience without being accountable to the same professional code as a real journalist.

But there are countless other bloggers who publish material every day and are not associated with any publication. Bloggers serve a similar purpose to journalists in that they gather information and package it for the public to read and consider—but often a blog is full of opinion and cannot be relied upon in the same way as a traditional news source.

Bloggers are different from journalists in that they are completely independent. They are not held to the same ethical standards as journalists, although many bloggers apply the same ethics of honesty and fairness to their work.

It's important for readers to keep this difference in mind when relying on bloggers to get news. The information that is posted and shared on blogs does not have to be edited or approved by anyone. It is not fact-checked, and sources are not verified by anyone other than the blogger. Individual people are able to speak for themselves only, rather than have their ideas represent a particular newspaper, organization, or political party.

Blogs are an interesting source for commentary, reflection, and opinion about current events. And the comments readers leave in response to a post are valuable additions to public discussion about a news story. There's no question that blogs serve an interesting and interactive role in how people understand the world today. But it's important to keep in mind how bloggers and journalists differ.

Chapter 3

The Rise of Citizen Journalism

Technology has blurred the lines between traditional journalism and public discourse, or discussion, about world events. Blogs and social media sites enable anyone to share with the world their ideas about politics, entertainment, culture, and sports; anyone can publish information and ideas on any topic. It can be difficult for a reader to know the source or the intention of this information.

The line between "official" journalism content and the sharing of a private citizen's content has been further blurred by the rise of what is called citizen journalism. Citizen journalism, also called participatory journalism, is a type of unofficial journalism in which private citizens—non-journalists—take part.

Cell phone technology and the Internet have made it possible for most anyone to record and share a story. If a person happens to be standing somewhere when something newsworthy happens, he or she can record or photograph it and share it with the world, almost instantly.

In recent years, this kind of so-called journalism—it is not an official type of journalism—has been increasing. Citizen journalism has been a

(Left to right): J. B. Hoston, president of NewsGator; Lee Alexander, citizen-journalism coordinator of news-record.com; Susan DeFife, president and CEO of Backfence.com; and Dan Gillmor, founder of Grassroots Media, Inc.

benefit to the sharing and understanding of news, but it can also be a little bit misleading.

Private Citizens Capturing the News

Perhaps a person is lucky enough to be in his or her local shopping mall when a famous pop singer shows up unexpectedly. The person's first response would probably be to take a photo or video of the event to share with friends. Or perhaps the same person sees a building in his or her town that is on fire; it might be interesting to make a video of that kind of news-worthy event, too.

These are both examples of happenings that, not long ago, people relied on professional news crews to photograph or videotape in order for the public to see them. But it is hard for a news crew to be everywhere all the time; journalists have to hear about an event and then get to the location as soon as possible, along with their cameras and other equipment. It's far faster to have a person who just happens to be where news is taking place capture live images. All you need is a phone with a camera, and to share your footage, you just need an Internet connection.

From wars to natural disasters, from sports events to gossip stories involving the rich and famous, private citizens have been covering it all. In some cases, traditional news sources have welcomed the participation of the public in recording the news. For example, CNN's iReport encourages people to join what it calls a global community of people who are passionate about the news.

Viewers can contribute images, videos, and audio files, and of course text, about virtually anything they deem interesting and newsworthy. CNN does not edit the content, nor does it verify that it is factual. That is an important difference between this type of citizen journalism and journalism that is practiced by reporters who are employed by CNN. That's just one example of a mainstream news source using footage recorded by private citizens in its reporting.

Benefits and Potential Pitfalls of Citizen Journalism

Citizen journalism means more people are participating in recording and sharing news. But it goes beyond that. Citizen journalism allows people to affect the actual content of the news, to have a say in what events get the attention of the mainstream news and people around the world. People no longer have to rely on traditional news sources to decide that a story is worth investigating and sharing in order for it to be shared.

This changes who decides what is "news." It provides a way for more voices to be heard. It used to be a select few editors could determine what stories got the most attention. Now the public can decide what they care about most and what news matters most. Of course, with so much content available online, it can be hard to filter through all of it. But if there's an issue or event that is interesting to you, you can be sure it's being covered by someone, somewhere.

On the other hand, it can be hard to know what news you can trust. Citizen journalists don't have to be as objective as professional journalists. They can tell stories from their point of view and share content that attempts to convince viewers or readers to feel a certain way or have a particular viewpoint on the story being told.

Seeing a disturbing, violent image from a war zone may trigger emotions in the viewer, but it does not give any real background information on what is actually taking place. To understand the news and develop your own ideas and opinions, you need to know context—what is happening, by whom, where, and why. Professional journalists are trained and committed to research and gather this information. Private citizens are not.

- □ X

File   Edit   View   Favorites   Tools   Help

MEDIA AND THE OCCUPY MOVEMENT

Media and the Occupy Movement

The Occupy movement is another example of citizen journalism creating a stir and making a real difference. The Occupy movement began in New York City in September 2011. Its participants were protesting how wealth is shared—their message was that the way our economic system works today, most of the wealth is given to a very small group of people, while the majority of people have far less. What began in New York has since spread all over the world, with similar protests happening in cities everywhere.

The movement did not get a lot of attention at first from mainstream news sources. Instead, it was through social media and other user-generated sites that the movement got attention and became more popular.

Citizen Journalists Making a Difference

Sites such as Facebook, Twitter, and YouTube are platforms for anyone to use to share information. In recent years, the impact of the information shared has been enormous. One example is the use of these sites and cell phone technologies in getting support for protests of citizens against their governments in the Middle East—called the Arab Spring, which began in 2010.

These protests forced leaders in countries including Yemen, Egypt, Tunisia, and Libya to be removed from office. Because traditional news media, particularly from Western countries like the United States, have difficulty getting permission to cover news stories in some of these countries, most of the images broadcast and shared came from citizen journalists in affected countries.

The Arab Spring has been called a social media revolution because of the enormous role social media played in capturing and spreading the word about what was happening and why. Without these resources,

Anti-government protesters shout during a rally organized by the Moroccan Arab Spring movement in February 2011. The instant distribution of such images worldwide enhanced awareness and support for all Arab Spring protests.

the world may not have known about the protests, and the protests may not have had such a great impact.

Citizenside (citizenside .com) is an example of an online platform for nonprofessional "journalists" to share video and photos of events they consider newsworthy.

The site, as well as others, has been an important tool for the Occupy movement, allowing a way for participants and observers of the protests to tell a story they felt was not being reported enough in the mainstream news. The site does fact-check its content—it verifies that a video or photo was taken at a real event. In this way, people who view content on the site know that it is authentic, or that what is

In the United States and eventually worldwide, the Occupy Wall Street movement expressed dissatisfaction with the way wealth is distributed. The movement gained momentum online and was eventually covered by traditional news media as well.

being shown actually happened. But this is not the same as being objective, or telling the story without bias, which is the goal of a professional journalist.

Neither the Arab Spring nor the Occupy movement could have been covered in the same way in the days before citizen journalism. Without the available and affordable technology, the speed of the Internet, and the growing interest the public has in participating in and finding alternative news sources, these stories and others may have reached a smaller audience, and the events may have had a much smaller impact.

Chapter 4

Weeding Truth from Slant, Bias, and Spin to Form Your Own Ideas

Journalists, bloggers, and citizen journalists all have something in common: they gather information in various formats—text, video, audio, photographic—and share it with the public. People similarly share their ideas by commenting on online news stories or posting to social networking sites like Facebook or Twitter, but it is more clear to the reader that these are opinions and not necessarily reliable facts.

It can be harder to distinguish the work of journalists, bloggers, and citizen journalists, but they differ in the kind of bias, slant, or spin they can include in their work. Here are definitions of these terms to help readers tell the difference between proper journalism and the less fair and balanced kind.

Bias, Slant, and Spin

The inclusion of bias, slant, and spin is important for a reader to be able to detect in a printed news story or video feature or photograph. They are all words that mean the writer or videographer or photographer had a particular viewpoint about the subject that he or she wants the reader or viewer to share.

Professional journalists are supposed to be impartial. That means the work they produce cannot represent one side of a story over another. Bias means favoring one viewpoint or side of an argument. Bloggers and citizen journalists can do this, and often they do. For example, if a person is living in a violent neighborhood and believes the police should do more to protect the nonviolent residents, he might produce a video or write a news story that focuses on innocent victims of violent crime. The purpose of the story would be to convince other people of the citizen journalist's or

A professional journalist, unlike a blogger or citizen journalist, is bound by a professional code to investigate all sides of a story and to deliver reports that are unbiased and balanced.

blogger's point of view, that the police should do more to protect the innocent residents of the particular neighborhood.

The reporting may be accurate and the argument may be valid, but the person preparing and sharing the story is showing bias because only one side of the story is being presented. A professional journalist, on the other hand, would be expected to talk not only to innocent residents who have been victims of crime but also to the local police chief and perhaps the mayor to discuss what work the police are doing to protect people and what challenges they face in solving crime in the neighborhood. That would be balanced reporting.

Slant is a little more subtle, or hard to detect, than bias. Slant is a way of reporting a story with bias in a way that tries not to be too obvious. Sometimes a choice of words can introduce slant to a story. For example, if you say a suspect was captured rather than picked up for questioning, it makes the person sound a little more dangerous and a little guiltier. This would be a subtle way for a reporter to slant the story toward her point of view, that the person is dangerous and guilty.

Spinning a story means adding or omitting facts to draw a conclusion that isn't entirely accurate. Spin is very similar to propaganda, in that it manipulates facts in order to shape public opinion on a subject. Talk radio personalities like Rush Limbaugh often use these techniques to get listeners to interpret news stories their way.

Professional journalists agree that they will not incorporate bias, slant, or spin into their work, although some newspapers and cable news channels are generally more liberal or conservative in their approach to news. Still, a journalist must be objective. Bloggers or citizen journalists do not have to be objective. That is not to say that they lie or that their contributions are not valuable and well researched, but as a reader or consumer of blog and

File   Edit   View   Favorites   Tools   Help

READING FROM MANY SOURCES

Reading from Many Sources

Read as much news from as many sources as you can to broaden your understanding. When we read news in our country, we read about things from only our country's point of view. The Internet allows us to see what people in other parts of the world are experiencing. True literacy is informing yourself of the facts and then establishing your own opinions about them. The Internet is a wonderful tool for doing both.

citizen journalism content, you must be alert to bias, slant, and spin to know how much you can trust what you read.

A Challenge for Readers

There is more than one truth. In a simpler world, there would be one right answer and one wrong one, there would be good people and bad people, and it would be clear which was which. But things are more complex. The factors that lead our leaders to make certain decisions—from school lunch cafeteria choices to whether our country should go to war—are complicated and interconnected.

Journalists help us understand these factors by looking at stories from different angles. Bloggers and citizen journalists often help us understand the issues of the world by more deeply and personally exposing people who are impacted by

A laptop is all anyone needs to publish what may or may not be researched, balanced, factual stories. A reader has to determine how reliable a blog post or piece of citizen journalism is.

events. It is a fantastic time to be a curious consumer of news because there is so much content available to inform the public.

But nobody wants to merely receive news and accept it as absolute truth. Being a thinking, literate person means gathering the information you read or view and processing it to come up with your own ideas. As a reader, your challenge is to filter through all the available content on a topic and formulate your own opinion. To do so, it is OK to read heavily biased stories about a topic, as long as you read stories that are heavily biased from all sides and not just one.

MYTHS & FACTS

MYTH Anything that is published, on the Web or elsewhere, is trustworthy and true.

FACT Because anyone with a computer is able to publish any content they wish, it is very important for a reader to consider the source of the information found online. Unless something has been verified, fact-checked, and sufficiently supported, it should not be relied upon as credible information. This is especially important to keep in mind when citing sources for research papers, but it's also important to remember when reading to inform yourself of current events.

MYTH

Content published on blogs is unreliable and is intended only to manipulate the reader into agreeing with the writer.

FACT

It is not true that all information on blogs is unreliable, but a savvy reader should be on the lookout for blog content that is supported by references to sources of information included, such as statistics, quotes, and other facts. The more a blogger supports his or her statements, the more reliable he or she is. Readers should also be able to detect language that indicates the writer is stating an opinion rather than an established fact. Opinions are also valuable to read and consider. One of the most fundamental features of social media, like blogs, is that readers can exchange ideas and opinions through posts and comments.

MYTH

If a story really matters, it will be covered by the traditional media. Otherwise, it can't be that important.

FACT

Traditional media sources—such as newspapers that have been around for decades or broadcast news programs with sky-high ratings—are no longer the only providers of news. In fact, many newspapers have had to shut down because fewer people are relying on them to get information. In recent cases, such as with the Arab Spring and the rise of the Occupy movement, it was actually non-journalists who first "broke" the stories by posting material online, which the traditional media outlets then used to base their initial coverage on.

Chapter 5

Online Content and the Law

Professional journalists are bound to particular ethical standards. Bloggers and other online news content providers who are not professional journalists are not bound by the same codes of practice, which gives them more freedom to publish and share content that is not necessarily balanced and fair in scope.

However, professional journalists are also legally protected in ways that bloggers and unofficial content publishers are not. The laws are in place to help journalists do their jobs more effectively. Because most laws were created in times when radio and print were the only news media, newer media like Web sites and blogs are not included in the definition of journalism as stated in the laws.

Shield Laws

Some states have what are called shield laws, which basically means a reporter does not have to reveal a source—a person he or she spoke with while investigating a story—in court. If a journalist does not have to reveal the names of every person he or she talks to during the research of a story, more people will probably be willing to talk to the journalist.

Although there is no federal law in the United States that says a journalist can protect a person who was a source for a story, federal judges will most often not force a journalist to reveal his or her sources. In some cases, where the source in question is involved in something illegal or is key to solving a bigger case, a reporter will be forced by the court to reveal the identity of the person, in which case the reporter can be fined or even jailed for refusing.

Forty states and the District of Columbia currently have shield laws. Idaho, Iowa, Massachusetts, Mississippi, Missouri, New Hampshire, South Dakota, Vermont, Virginia, and Wyoming do not. Many people believe

There are laws to protect journalists from having to reveal sources. *New York Times* reporter Judith Miller was jailed for 85 days for refusing to name a source. These laws don't protect citizen journalists or bloggers.

there should be a federal shield law for journalists, but those against it say that no citizen of the United States should be able to ignore a court order to reveal information that is important to solving a crime or protecting national security.

Bloggers are not protected by shield laws. In 2011, Crystal Cox, a self-proclaimed investigative blogger in Oregon, made statements on her blog about an attorney, whom she called a "thug" and a "thief" in a story about a particular case on which the attorney had worked. The attorney sued Cox for defamation of character—which means he accused her of publishing untrue statements about him that hurt his reputation. The only way to disprove a defamation case is to prove that the statements made were in fact true. In Cox's case, she did not want to reveal the sources that had told her the attorney had acted criminally during a particular case, and the judge ruled that she was not a journalist, had no formal journalistic training, and was not affiliated with a particular media outlet, and therefore she was not protected by the state's shield laws.

Retraction Statutes

Retraction statutes are laws that protect a journalist, publication, or news broadcaster from being sued for libel. Libel is when something untrue and damaging about a person is published or broadcasted. In such cases, the person who has been libeled can sue for damages.

Retraction statutes allow the reporter or media company responsible for the libel to retract, or take back, the untrue statements, by printing or other-wise sharing in a clear and obvious manner a correction to what had been said. If an untrue statement is retracted in a timely manner, a libel suit can be avoided.

This is important protection for journalists and media outlets to have. Not all libel is intentional or done to cause damage. Journalists are human and make mistakes. Often journalists and editors are working quickly to make a deadline, which makes it even more likely that some errors make it through to publication (although, as professionals, journalists and editors are

Public figures are covered by some form of news media. When anyone with a telephone can distribute images and stories around the world, it can be hard to protect one's privacy.

expected to get things right the vast majority of the time!). As long as these mistakes are acknowledged and corrected in a timely manner, these instances can be resolved without lawsuits.

Redefining Journalism

Given that these laws and protections were established to allow journalists to do their jobs without fear of legal difficulty, should nontraditional journalists be protected also? This is a big question that is currently being debated in news media circles.

FREE FLOW OF INFORMATION ACT

File   Edit   View   Favorites   Tools   Help

Free Flow of Information Act

So what is a journalist? In a March 2012 case, a proposed state law called the Free Flow of Information Act seems to include bloggers in its definition of what is journalism and what should therefore be covered by the state's shield laws. The bill states that:

"[A]ny newspaper, magazine or other periodical, book publisher, news agency, wire service, radio or television station or network, cable or satellite station or network, or audio or audiovisual production company, or any entity that is in the regular business of news gathering and disseminating news or information to the public by any means, including, but not limited to, print, broadcast, photographic, mechanical, internet, or electronic distribution."

Lawmakers on the state and federal level have been debating whether shield laws, which were written with only official print journalists in mind, should also protect bloggers.

Those who are opposed to nontraditional journalists—including bloggers and citizen journalists—being protected by these laws say a person is not practicing official journalism if he or she is not working for an established media outlet. But others argue that the practice of journalism itself, not the person, is what is protected by laws. Even if a person is not officially a "journalist," if what he or she is doing is considered "journalism," then the work should be protected.

There is no doubt that the Internet and other technology is changing how we learn, how we share, and how we experience current events. But how these new methods fit with the more traditional definitions of journalism and what status to give to information that is gathered and shared by nontraditional journalists and media outlets is a complicated question.

TEN GREAT QUESTIONS

TO ASK A BLOGGER

1 What is your blog mostly about?

2 What do you hope to accomplish with your blog?

3 Do you consider yourself a journalist?

4 How much research do you do for your posts?

5 What kind of feedback do you hope to receive?

6 How are blogs different from and the same as traditional media?

7 What do you feel is your responsibility to your readers?

8 What is a blogger's role in society?

9 Do you think bloggers should be objective, like journalists?

10 Should bloggers have the same legal protection as journalists?

GLOSSARY

accountability A journalist's responsibility to the public to report factually.

alternative media Media sources that are outside mainstream media.

bias A prejudice or set idea about a topic or group of people.

blog A Web log on which content is published on a particular topic.

blogger A person who writes or maintains a blog.

citizen journalist A private person who acts as a journalist by sharing video, photo, or written content about a news event.

ethics A set of moral rules or standards.

journalist A person whose job it is to gather and report on news events.

libel The publication of something that is untrue about a person or organization that causes damage to the reputation of the subject.

objective Not influenced by personal feelings or bias.

online newspaper A newspaper or edition of a newspaper that is published online versus on paper.

plagiarism The act of copying or heavily borrowing another person's work without giving credit.

retraction The taking back or correction of something that has been published that is not true.

shield laws Laws that protect journalists from having to reveal sources.

slant In journalism, reporting a story with bias.

social media Interactive Web and mobile phone technologies that allow people to share comments and opinions.

source A person a journalist talks to when gathering information for a news story.

spin The manipulation of facts to draw a conclusion in a news story that isn't entirely accurate.

traditional media Media that existed before the Internet, such as newspapers, radio, television, and books.

tweet A message of 140 characters or less that a person posts via Twitter, a social media site.

FOR MORE INFORMATION

American Press Institute
4401 Wilson Boulevard, Suite 900
Arlington, VA 22203
(571) 366-1195
Web site: http://www.americanpressinstitute.org
The American Press Institute educates constituencies about the value of
    newspapers and provides training, research, and best practices
    for newspaper industry executives.

Common Sense Media
650 Townsend, Suite 435
San Francisco, CA 94103
(415) 863-0600
Web site: http://www.commonsensemedia.org
This organization is dedicated to providing trustworthy information, education,
    and an independent voice in the world of media and technology.

Online News Association
P.O. Box 65741
Washington, DC 20035
(646) 290-7900
Web site: http://journalists.org
The Online News Association is a nonprofit membership organization for
    digital journalists, connecting journalism, technology, and innovation.

Project for Excellence in Journalism (PEJ)
1615 L Street NW 700
Washington, DC 20036
(202) 419-3650

Web site: http://www.journalism.org/about_pej/about_us
PEJ is an organization dedicated to trying to understand the information
    revolution.

Society of Professional Journalists
Eugene S. Pulliam National Journalism Center
3909 N. Meridian Street
Indianapolis, IN 46208
(317) 927-8000
Web site: http://www.spj.org
The Society of Professional Journalists is dedicated to the perpetuation of a
    free press as the cornerstone of our nation and our liberty.

Web Sites

Due to the changing nature of Internet links, Rosen Publishing has developed
an online list of Web sites related to the subject of this book. This site is
updated regularly. Please use this link to access the list:

http://www.rosenlinks.com/DIL/Press

FOR FURTHER READING

Associated Press. *The Associated Press Stylebook and Briefing on Media Law 2011*. New York, NY: Basic Books, 2011.

Barr, Chris. *The Yahoo! Style Guide: The Ultimate Sourcebook for Writing, Editing, and Creating Content for the Digital World*. New York, NY: St. Martin's Griffin, 2010.

Briggs, Mark. *Entrepreneurial Journalism*. Kindle ed. Washington, DC: CQ Press, 2011.

Briggs, Mark. *Journalism Next: A Practical Guide to Digital Reporting and Publishing*. Washington, DC: CQ Press, 2009.

Cappon, Rene. *The Associated Press Guide to News Writing: The Resource for Professional Journalists*. New York, NY: Basic Books, 1999.

Cappon, Rene. *The Associated Press Guide to Punctuation*. New York, NY: Basic Books, 2003.

Felder, Lynda. *Writing for the Web*. Berkeley, CA: New Riders Press, 2011.

Grappone, Jennifer. *Search Engine Optimization (SEO): An Hour a Day*. Alameda, CA: Sybex, 2011.

Gunelius, Susan M. *Blogging All in One for Dummies*. Hoboken, NJ: Wiley, 2010.

Higbee, Tristan. *101 Blogging Tips*. Kindle ed. TheBackLight.com, 2010.

Kerpen, Dave. *Likeable Social Media: How to Delight Your Customers, Create an Irresistible Brand, and Be Generally Amazing on Facebook (And Other Social Networks)*. New York, NY: McGraw-Hill, 2011.

Knight, Robert M. *Journalistic Writing: Building the Skills, Honing the Craft*. Portland, OR: Marion Street Press, 2010.

Luckie, Mark S. *The Digital Journalist's Handbook*. CreateSpace: Amazon.com, 2010.

Martin, Gail. *30 Days to Social Media Success: The 30 Day Results Guide to Making the Most of Twitter, Blogging, LinkedIn, and Facebook*. Pompton Plains, NJ: Career Press, 2010.

O'Reilly, Tim, and Sarah Milstein. *The Twitter Book*. Sebastopol, CA: O'Reilly Media, 2011.

Passante, Christopher K. *The Complete Idiot's Guide to Journalism*. New York, NY: Alpha Books, 2007.

Schaefer, Mark W. *The Tao of Twitter: Changing Your Life and Business 140 Characters at a Time*. New York: McGraw-Hill, 2011.

Siegal, Allan M., and William G. Connolly. *The New York Times Manual of Style and Usage*. New York, NY: Three Rivers Press, 2002.

Stovall, James Glen. *Web Journalism: Practice and Promise of a New Medium*. Upper Saddle River, NJ: Pearson Education, 2003.

Thornburg, Robert M. *Producing Online News: Digital Skills, Stronger Stories*. Washington, DC: CQ Press, 2010.

Wright-Porto, Heather. *Creative Blogging: Your First Steps to a Successful Blog*. New York, NY: Apress, 2011.

BIBLIOGRAPHY

Barnard, Jeff. "Montana Blogger Sued for Defamation Not a Journalist, Judge Rules." *Law Technology News.* Law.com, December 9, 2011. Retrieved February 8, 2012 (http://www.law.com/jsp/lawtechnologynews/PubArticleLTN.jsp?id=1202534942743&slreturn=1).

Benson, Jonathan. "Distrust in Mainstream Media Nears All Time High." NaturalNews.com. October 3, 2010. Retrieved February 28, 2012 (http://www.naturalnews.com/029931_distrust_mainstream_media.htmlgo).

Bunz, Mercedes. "Old Media or New Media—Who Breaks the News Today?" *Guardian*, January 12, 2010. Retrieved March 3, 2012 (http://www.guardian.co.uk/media/pda/2010/jan/12/digital-media-hyperlocal-media-baltimore-pew-study).

Carr, David. "Reporting on a Scarcity of Reporting Without Reporting." *New York Times*, January 11, 2010. Retrieved March 3, 2012 (http://mediadecoder.blogs.nytimes.com/2010/01/11/reporting-on-a-scarcity-of-reporting-without-reporting).

Farley, John. "Jailed for Covering the Wall Street Protests." Salon.com, September 28, 2011. Retrieved February 24, 2012 (http://www.salon.com/2011/09/28/wall_street_protest_arrested).

Fritz, Ben. "Most Original News Reporting Comes from Traditional Sources, Study Finds." *Los Angeles Times*, January 11, 2010. Retrieved March 1, 2012 (http://articles.latimes.com/2010/jan/11/business/la-fi-ct-newspapers11-2010jan11).

Gupta, Arun. "Occupy's Challenge: Reinventing Democracy." Salon.com, February 27, 2010. Retrieved March 1, 2012 (http://www.salon.com/2012/02/27/occupys_challenge_reinventing_democracy).

Journalism.org. "How Blogs and Social Media Agendas Relate and Differ from the Traditional Press." May 23, 2010. Retrieved February 16, 2012 (http://www.journalism.org/analysis_report/new_media_old_media).

Kovach, Bill. *The Elements of Journalism*. New York, NY: Three Rivers Press, 2007.

Lieberman, David. "Newspaper Closings Raise Fears About Industry." *USA Today*, March 19, 2009. Retrieved January 30, 2012 (http://www.usatoday.com/money/media/2009-03-17-newspapers-downturn_N.htm).

Marsh, Kevin. "End of Journalism as We Know It." *Guardian*, January 4, 2010. Retrieved March 12, 2012 (http://www.guardian.co.uk/commentisfree/2010/jan/04/citizenmedia-bbc).

Marshall, Sarah. "Citizen Journalism, Cyber Censorship and the Arab Spring." Journalism.co.uk, March 12, 2012. Retrieved March 14, 2012 (http://www.journalism.co.uk/news-features/citizen-journalism-cyber-censorship-arab-spring/s5/a548289).

New York Times. "Are All Bloggers Journalists?" Room for Debate, *New York Times*, December 11, 2011. Retrieved February 11, 2012 (http://www.nytimes.com/roomfordebate/2011/12/11/are-all-bloggers-journalists).

Preston, Jennifer. "Protesters Look for Ways to Feed the Web." *New York Times*, November 24, 2011. Retrieved February 10, 2012 (http://www.nytimes.com/2011/11/25/business/media/occupy-movement-focuses-on-staying-current-on-social-networks.html).

Rogers, Tony. "The Basics of Libel and Libel Law." About.com. Retrieved January 30, 2012 (http://journalism.about.com/od/ethicsprofessionalism/a/libel.htm).

Schillenger, Raymond. "Social Media and the Arab Spring: What Have We Learned?" Huffington Post, September 20, 2011. Retrieved February 29, 2012 (http://www.huffingtonpost.com/raymond-schillinger/arab-spring-social-media_b_970165.html).

Society of Professional Journalists. "SPJ'S Code of Ethics." Retrieved February 10, 2012 (http://www.spj.org/ethicscode.asp).

Society of Professional Journalists. "Struggling to Report: The Fight for a Federal Shield Law." Retrieved February 20, 2012 (http://www.spj .org/shieldlaw.asp).

Taylor, Kate. "Arab Spring Was Social Media Revolution." *TG Daily*, September 13, 2011. Retrieved March 5, 2012 (http://www.tgdaily.com/ software-features/58426-arab-spring-really-was-social-media-revolution).

Walsh, Erin. "Cyber Journalism and the Future of New Media." Las Vegas International Press Club, June 24, 2011. Retrieved February 1, 2012 (http://lvpressclub.com/journalism/cyber-journalism-and-the-future- of-new-media).

Wassom, Brian. "5 Predictions for Social Media Law in 2012." Mashable Social Media, January 5, 2012. Retrieved January 12, 2012 (http:// mashable.com/2012/01/05/social-media-legal-predictions).

About the Author

Tracy Brown studied journalism at Emerson College and the European Institute for International Communication and has written several books for young adults on a variety of topics. She lives in the Netherlands.

Photo Credits

Cover, pp. 1 (left), 11 Christopher Robbins/Photodisc/Thinkstock; cover, pp. 1 (middle left), 15 Ethan Miller/Getty Images; cover, pp. 1 (middle right), 5 Vincent Dolman/Digital Vision/Getty Images; cover, p. 1 (right) © iStockphoto.com/Arda Guldogan; p. 7 Raleigh News & Observer/McClatchy-Tribune/Getty Images; p. 9 mediaphotos/the Agency Collection/Getty Images; p. 14 Dan Kitwood/Getty Images; p. 18 © The Toronto Star/ZUMA Press; pp. 21, 24, 33, 36 © AP Images; p. 25 Emmanuel Dunand/AFP/Getty Images; p. 27 Digital Vision/Thinkstock; p. 29 Fabrizio Cacciatore/Photolibrary/Getty Images; p. 35 Paul Bradbury/OJO Images/Getty Images; cover (background) and interior page graphics © iStockphoto.com/suprun.

Designer: Nicole Russo; Editor: Bethany Bryan;
Photo Researcher: Karen Huang